Welcome to Father Time!

One of the first important lessons that I learned when I became a new dad was that my child would need my love, nurturance and support "around the clock." Indeed, good dads engage their kids physically, emotionally and spiritually. In a practical sense, that means that they provide, nurture and guide their children. Truly, the rewarding work of being a dad is never done. It's an exhilarating "24/7" commitment that challenges every dad to be the best dad that he can be. That's why I am so excited about our **24/7 Dad**™ program. It provides the around the clock support that every dad needs.

24/7 Dad™ is a unique and innovative fatherhood program developed by a team of nationally and internationally recognized fathering experts and fatherhood practitioners. The **24/7 Dad**™ program focuses on characteristics that every father needs and covers the universal aspects of fatherhood so that men of all cultures, races, religions, and backgrounds can benefit from the program. You will hone your fathering skills as you learn about yourself and the important roles that you have with your children and in your family. In addition, you will learn important ways to strengthen your relationship with your wife or with the mother of your children. Finally, you will be given a great opportunity to develop effective strategies to manage your physical and mental health and to help you balance your work and family commitments.

When I said that the **24/7 Dad**™ program was comprehensive, I wasn't kidding. But it needs to be. After all, the health and well-being of your children is at stake. (Frankly, I am a bit envious that a fathering program like this was not available before I changed my first diaper!) So wind your "fatherhood time piece" and get ready to embark on the exciting and rewarding journey—the journey to become a 24/7 dad. And always remember that "father time is all the time when you are somebody's dad!"

Best regards,

Roland C. Warren

Roland Warren
President
National Fatherhood Initiative

To Learn More About NFI and the *24/7 Dad*™ Programs:

LEARN MORE ABOUT NATIONAL FATHERHOOD INITIATIVE

101 Lake Forest Boulevard, Suite 360
Gaithersburg, MD 20877

Phone: (301) 948-0599
Fax: (301) 948-4325
Email: info@fatherhood.org
Website: www.fatherhood.org

National Fatherhood Initiative℠

First Edition
John Chacón, Karen Patterson and Christopher Brown
With contributions from Stephen Bavolek, Ph.D., CEO & Founder of Family Development Resources, Inc.

© 2003 National Fatherhood Initiative   Printed in the United States of America.

ATTENTION: Trademark and Copyright Protection
The manuals, inventories and other instructional materials published by the National Fatherhood Initiative are federally protected against unauthorized reproduction whether print or electronic.

Dads Club™

You're a dad for life, so join the Dads Club™ for life!

SHOW YOUR COMMITMENT. JOIN THE CLUB.
Show your commitment to involved, responsible, and committed fatherhood by becoming a lifetime member of Dads Club™. Give a one-time gift of $30, and you'll receive an exclusive T-shirt, CD-ROM, and more exciting resources!

Call (301) 948-0599 or visit www.fatherhood.org.

FREE! Dad E-mail

Hints, tips, and how to's for dads!

Delivered Wednesdays straight to your inbox.

Get connected today at www.fatherhood.org.

WE'RE LOOKING FOR A FEW GOOD MEN...
★★★ TO DO ★★★
DOUBLE DUTY!

DOUBLE DUTY DAD

The Double Duty Dad™ program aims to give experienced fathers a chance to mentor fatherless children and less experienced dads.

★ ★ ★ ★ ★ ★ ★ ★ ★ ★ ★ ★ ★ ★ ★ ★ ★

With just 24 hours a year, you can make a huge difference in the life of a child!

★ ★ ★ ★ ★ ★ ★ ★ ★ ★ ★ ★ ★ ★ ★ ★ ★

To learn more about how you can help, visit
www.doubledutydad.org

FATHER SOURCE
The Fatherhood Resource Center
www.fathersource.org | 301-948-0599

Wondering how to balance work and family? Want to help your child succeed in school? We can help!
Visit www.fathersource.org today.

24:7 A.M. Dad
FATHERING HANDBOOK

National Fatherhood Initiative

24/7 Dad A.M.™ Program

FATHERING HANDBOOK

TABLE OF CONTENTS

I.	Session 1 Family of Origin	1
II.	Session 2 Masculinity	5
III.	Session 3 Understanding Yourself	10
IV.	Session 4 Handling and Expressing Emotions	14
V.	Session 5 Spirituality	18
VI.	Session 6 Physical and Mental Health	22
VII.	Session 7 Fathering and Family Roles	26
VIII.	Session 8 Fathering and Culture	30
IX.	Session 9 Discipline, Rewards and Punishment	34
X.	Session 10 Expectations and Children's Development	40
XI.	Session 11 Balancing Work and Family	42
XII.	Session 12 Getting Involved With Your Children	48
XIII.	Parent Sessions	52
XIV.	Appendix Ages and Stages	i

Session 1
Family of Origin

When I was growing up, the role of the father in the family was _____
_____
_____.

I believe the role a father should have in the family today is _____
_____
_____.

The primary role I have in my family is _____
_____
_____.

Roles that my wife (partner) shares equally with me are _____
_____
_____.

One role I refuse to do is _____
_____.
because _____
_____
_____.

The *24/7 Dad A.M.*™ program is based on the five traits of the ideal father.

Self-Awareness

The 24/7 Dad is aware of himself as a man and aware of how important he is to his family. He is in touch with his moods, feelings, and emotions. He knows his strengths and limits. The 24/7 Dad takes responsibility for his own actions and knows that his growth depends on how well he knows and accepts himself.

The 24/7 Dad asks himself:
"How well am I doing in knowing myself?"

Caring for Self

The 24/7 Dad takes care of himself. He goes for yearly check-ups, eats the right foods, exercises, and learns new facts about the world he lives in. He has a strong spiritual connection to his community and chooses friends that support his healthy choices. The 24/7 Dad models behaviors for his children that clearly show he respects and likes himself by making good choices.

The 24/7 Dad asks himself:
"How well am I doing in taking care of myself?"

Fathering Skills

Fathering is a man's unique ability to contribute to the positive health and well-being of his children and family. The 24/7 Dad is very aware of the vital role he has in the family. He is a positive role model. He knows that fathers are involved in the daily life of their children. The 24/7 Dad gets his kids up, dressed and fed in the mornings. He meets with his children's teachers and helps his children with homework. He supports his children's interests in sports and other activities. The 24/7 Dad knows that he and the mother of his children parent differently. In other words, he knows the difference between "fathering" and "mothering" and how that difference is good for his children.

The 24/7 Dad asks himself:
"How well am I doing in being a Father?"

Parenting Skills

Parenting is the knowledge and skills that dads and moms need to raise healthy, happy children. The 24/7 Dad nurtures his children. He knows and accepts how vital his parenting skills are to developing the physical, emotional, intellectual, social, spiritual and creative needs of his children. The 24/7 Dad creates a positive, trusting home where children grow with the support and love of dad who cares for and nurtures them. A 24/7 Dad knows that discipline teaches and guides children, and is not used to physically and emotionally threaten or harm them.

The 24/7 Dad asks himself:
"How well am I doing in being a parent?"

Relationship Skills

The 24/7 Dad builds and maintains healthy relationships with his children, wife, family and friends and community. He knows and values the power of relationships to shape the characters of his children, and the quality of life he has with his wife. He knows that how well he communicates, models proper behavior, and chooses healthy friends all help shape the lives of his family.

The 24/7 Dad asks himself:
"How well am I doing in my relationships?"

Weekly Activity Log

Session 1: Family of Origin

a. One new thing I learned today was _____
_____
_____
_____

b. The reason this information will help me become a better dad is: _____
_____
_____
_____

Notes

Session 2
Masculinity

Looking back at my childhood and then at the things I do with my children, one way I wish my father had been different with me is _____
_____
_____.

I wish this because _____
_____
_____.

What does society expect of men that affects them in good and bad ways?

What is acceptable for a man or woman to be is based on how they are raised by their parents and the norms of culture.

What is acceptable for a man to be in any culture ranges from traditional to non-traditional. The traditional way that men are raised in many cultures teaches men both good and bad things about being a man.

a. Which characteristics of masculinity do you most identify with? _____
_____
_____.

b. Which characteristics are most important for a man to have in today's world? _____
_____
_____.

c. Have the characteristics of masculinity today changed from when you were a boy? _____
_____
_____.

d. Which characteristics do you least identify with? _____
_____
_____.

"Male Zones"

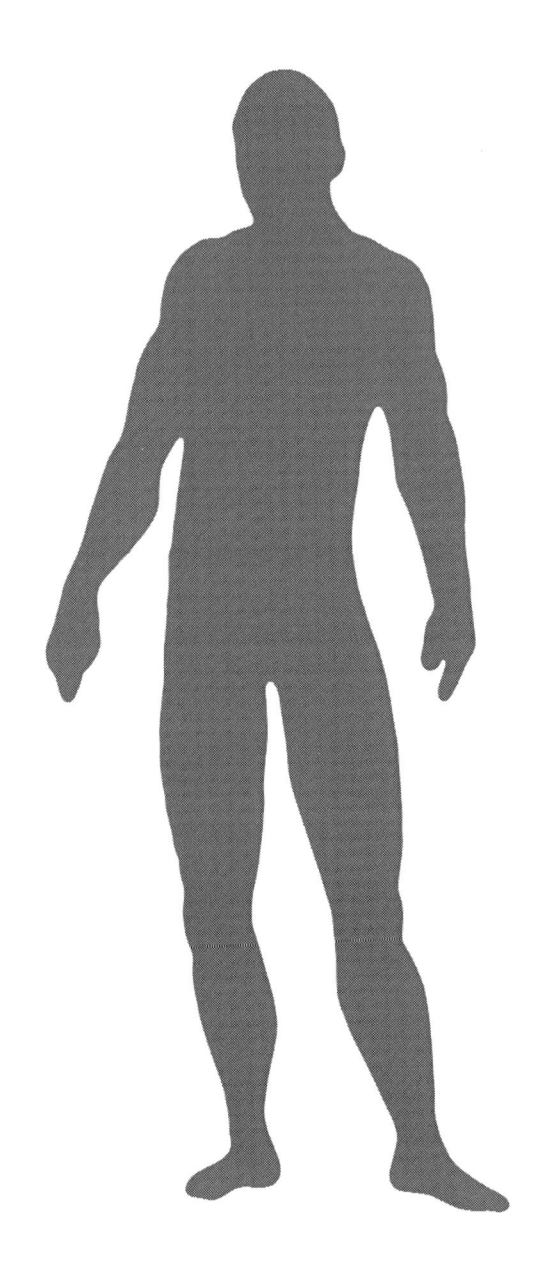

"Male Zones"

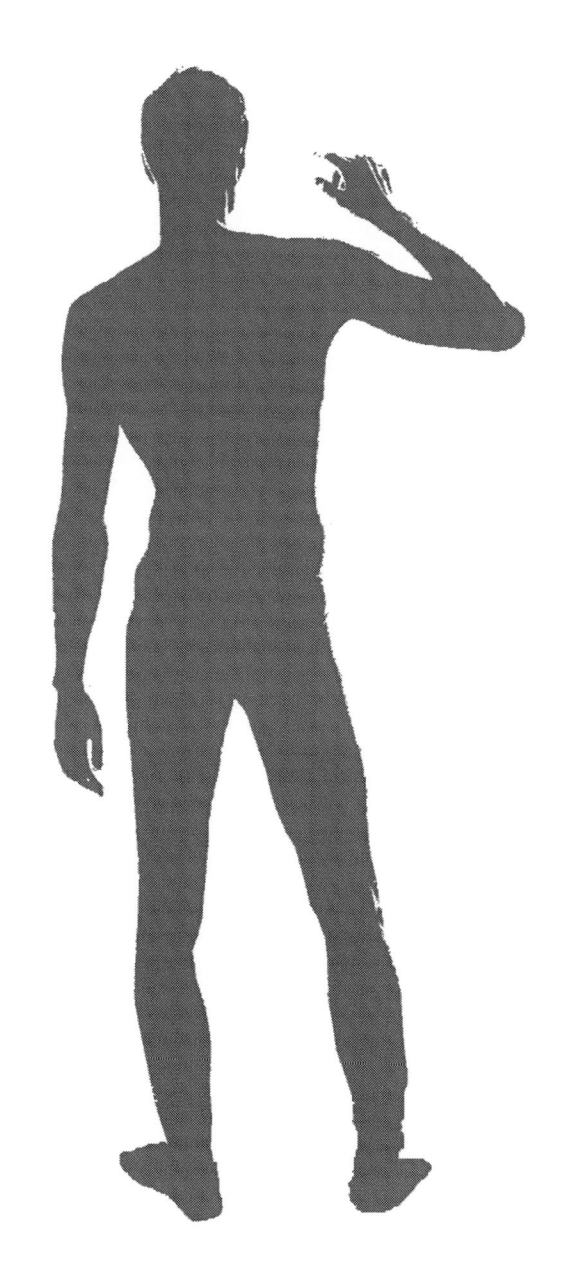

Weekly Activity Log

Session 2: Masculinity

a. One new thing I learned today was _____
_____
_____
_____

b. The reason this information will help me become a better dad is: _____
_____
_____
_____

Notes

Session 3
Understanding Your Self

When I think about myself, three traits that come to mind are _____

_____, and

_____

_____ .

About Me Inventory

1. One of my earliest childhood memories of being a little boy is _____

_____

_____ .

2. The influence my Dad had on me was:

    (Circle one):   Positive

                          Negative

                          About 50-50

3. The influence my mother had on me was:

    (Circle one):   Positive

                          Negative

                          About 50-50

4. What I learned about relationships watching my mom and dad was:

    a. Relationships between a husband and wife can be loving.

    b. Relationships between a husband and wife can be unsupportive and hurting.

    c. Children are a positive, not a negative part of the husband-wife relationship.

    d. Husbands are controlling and forceful.

    e. Wives are controlling and forceful.

    f. Other _____

_____

_____

Self-worth and Self-concept

Self-worth is a term used to describe the overall value a person has for himself.

Self-worth is made up of two components:

Self-concept

The **thoughts** a person has about himself. A self-concept can be positive or negative thoughts related to different aspects of a person's life. A person might have a positive self-concept of himself as a gardener, but a negative self-concept of himself as a cook. The self-concept of a person varies as widely as his roles and responsibilities. The person with an overall positive self-concept generally thinks of himself in a positive way.

Self-esteem

The **feelings** he has about himself. Overall, does a person hold himself in high esteem, or low esteem? Messages we get from others contribute greatly to our self-esteem.

One aspect of my life about which I have a **positive** self-concept is_____.

One aspect of my life about which I have a **negative** self-concept is _____.

The 24/7 Dad wants to improve his own self-worth, as well as the self-worth of his family.

To improve self-worth, try the following:

1. Position yourself and your family members for success. Nothing improves a low self-concept as quickly as success. Instead of pointing out how many wrong things you or your children do, point out how many right things happen.

2. Use praise to compliment yourself on who you are (your being) and on what you accomplish or try to accomplish (your doing).

My best quality is _____
_____.

3. Praise your children and other family members for just being the people they are; and praise them also for their accomplishments and overall positive behavior.

Praise for "Being"

"You are a wonderful son, and I feel proud being your father."

Praise for "Behavior"

"You did a great job cleaning your room."

Keeping the Praise for Being and Praise for Behavior separate gets rid of the "conditional" praise of "If you do this, then you are a good person." Example: You did a great job cleaning your room. Daddy really loves you," tells children that to receive praise they have to do something.

Praising a child for the wonderful person he or she is (Praise for Being), or for the good job he or she did (Praise for Behavior) helps children know that even when they mess up, Dad still loves them.

Steps to Using Praise

To praise properly, follow the steps below:

1. Focus your attention on your child. Let your child know he or she has your complete attention.

2. Move close to your child. A comfortable level of closeness makes the praise special.

3. Make eye contact with your child on the child's level. Stoop down to make eye contact with a small child.

4. Gently touch your child—touch is a positive form of communication.

5. Look pleasant—everyone likes to see a happy face.

6. Praise your child for being a great person or for their proper behavior.

7. Offer a hug to "seal" the nice words.

Weekly Activity Log

Session 3: Understanding Yourself

a. One new thing I learned today was _____
_____
_____
_____

b. The reason this information will help me become a better dad is: _____
_____
_____
_____

Notes

Session 4
Handling and Expressing Emotions

The message I received when I was a young boy about expressing feelings or showing emotions was _____
_____
_____.

One feeling I have trouble handling is _____
_____
_____.

When I feel _____, I usually behave _____
_____
_____.

Feelings and thoughts have energy. The energy that comes with each feeling and thought wants to be expressed.

Every experience we have also comes with thoughts and feelings. Memories are the thoughts about experiences in our past. Whether these memories are positive or negative depends on the experience. Good times provide us with good memories; bad or painful times provide us with bad memories.

A feeling is attached to every memory. We can label feelings as either feelings of comfort or discomfort. Referring to feelings in this way takes away the notion of some feelings being "bad" and some being "good." All feelings tell us something about an experience.

Men are raised from an early age not to express feelings and to keep them inside, especially feelings of discomfort. The result is the increase in physical and emotional problems men struggle with throughout their lives.

The more we cover up our feelings, the less freedom we have. The more experiences we cover up, the more energy it takes and the less growth we can make. Feelings of depression, stress or anger happen when we have so many feelings of discomfort that we use most of our energy to cover them up.

It's okay in some cases to suppress emotions. Men tend to control their emotions differently than women. And this is good in some cases. For example, it's okay to ignore fear in the face of danger when fear might keep you from taking action to protect your family. Men and women process emotions differently, and this is okay. The important thing for men to remember is to express their emotions in healthy ways.

Children and adults receive messages all their lives that only certain feelings are good and that the majority of feelings are bad. The fact is that all feelings are okay. It's the way we express feelings that can cause trouble. The same is true with the thoughts we have. All thoughts are okay. It's the way we act on our thoughts that counts.

There are two ways to express the energy of thoughts and feelings: proper and improper.

The 24/7 Dad follows the laws of Respect:

Respect Yourself - Don't behave in disrespectful ways to yourself.

Respect Others - Don't behave in disrespectful ways towards others.

Respect Your Environment - Don't behave in disrespectful ways towards the environment.

Grief and Loss

Feelings of grief and loss are perhaps the two feelings men have the most trouble handling and expressing. Other feelings men have trouble expressing appropriately are anger and stress.

Loss means to not have something any longer; to have something taken away by accident, carelessness, parting, or death.

Loss can refer to concrete items such as money, home, a person or a business, or to less concrete items such as love, health, status, or a game.

Grief is the response people have to loss in their lives. It includes many kinds of responses that vary with each person, the type of loss and its meaning to them, and their experiences.

Grieving is the process of coping with loss.
- Grieving allows people to find new ways of coping with loss.
- Grieving takes time, sometimes years.

Research suggests that men and women tend to grieve differently.
- Men tend not to care for their own emotions when they grieve. They hide their grief from others. In doing so, they neglect their emotional health.
- Men don't want to be seen to care too much about their emotional pain. Statements like, 'It doesn't hurt that bad" or "I'm okay" are common.
- Men tend to rely more on others (women, for example) to help them understand their own emotions and for emotional strength.
- Men tend to need privacy, may take time away or want to be alone to think things through.
- Men may show and express more anger.
- Men might not display their grief in public.
- Men grieve through ritual activities such as doing or making something.

When you grieve:
- Show courage. Allow yourself to experience grief rather than covering up your feelings.
- Communicate your need to be alone.
- Don't shut others out.
- Keep communication open.
- Tune into your body and become aware of how your body responds to grief.
- Use family rituals and activity to work through your grief.
- Slow down and reflect on the cause of your grief.
- Stay close to friends you can count on.
- Spend time outdoors.
- Stay in good health and exercise.

An experience of loss is expressed as grief (sadness).

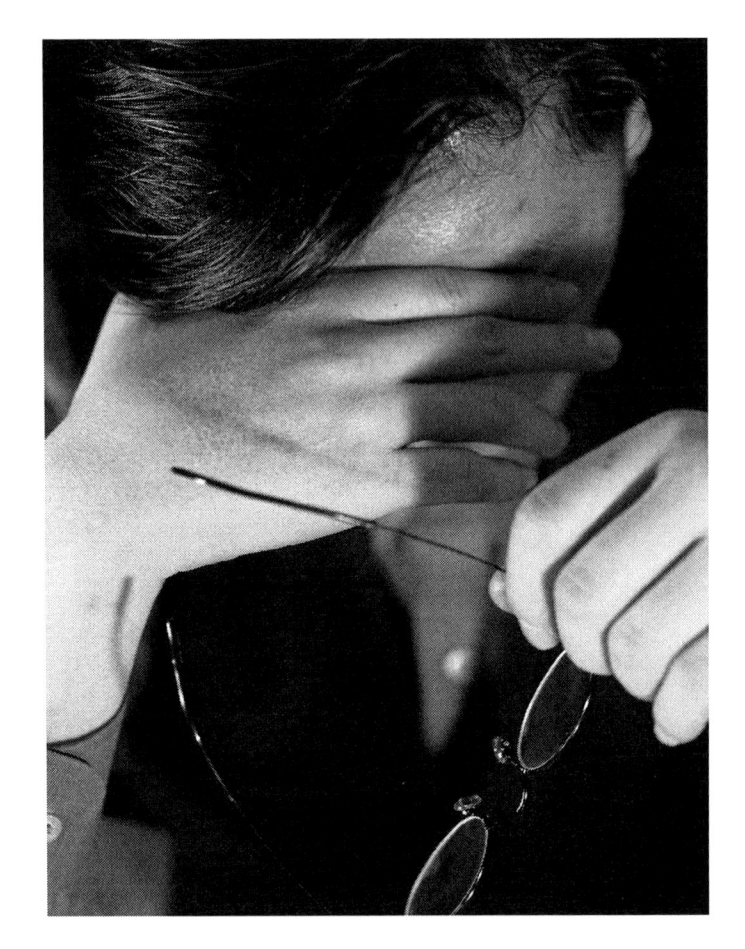

Describe an early experience of a loss and how you did or did not grieve: _____
_____
_____
_____
_____
_____
_____
_____.

What did you learn as a boy about the way to grieve? _____
_____
_____
_____
_____.

Are there "proper" and "improper" ways of grieving? _____
_____
_____
_____
_____.

Weekly Activity Log

Session 4: Handling and Expressing Emotions

a. One new thing I learned today was _____
_____
_____
_____.

b. The reason this information will help me become a better dad is: _____
_____
_____
_____

Session 5
Spirituality

To me, spirituality means _____
_____
_____
_____.

To me, a sense of spirituality is (or is not) important because _____
_____
_____
_____.

The word "spirituality" has to do with the spirit of the human soul:

- It is our moral, religious, or emotional nature as humans.
- It is the part of each person that feels a great attachment to, or part of someone or something else.
- It is a feeling of membership or belonging to a cause or group.
- It is the force of life that tries to find meaning and purpose.

Spirituality is love, it is kindness, it is caring, and it is also faith.

To me, spirituality means _____
_____
_____

and religion means _____
_____
_____.

Can people be spiritual and not religious? Religious and not spiritual? Religious and spiritual at the same time?

Spirituality is a part of who we are—just like our arms, legs, heads, etc. Religion is a set of rituals, traditions, and dogma that reflect certain beliefs about the universe, our place in it, and how we are linked to a higher power. Both can exist together and apart from one another.

Two ways I express my spirituality as a man are
_____
_____
and _____
_____
_____.

Two ways I express my spirituality as a father are
_____
_____
and _____
_____
_____.

Many people have noted over the years that spirituality is an important part of family. A "spiritual family" is one that feels all its members are part of the family, and each member feels that he or she belongs. The members of a "spiritual family" communicates with and cooperates, loves, and respects one another.

Rate your family spirituality in the categories below as your family "is today," and where you would like your family to be.

Family Spirituality Checklist

Use the following rating scale to respond to the statements.

    1 Very Weak   4 Above Average
    2 Somewhat   5 Very Strong
    3 Average

1. **Family members communicate with each other.**
    How we are today ____ We need to be ____

2. **Compliments are given freely.**
    How we are today ____ We need to be ____

3. **We touch each other in affection.**
    How we are today ____ We need to be ____

4. **We do things together as a family.**
    How we are today ____ We need to be ____

5. **Family members feel free to negotiate and compromise.**
    How we are today ____ We need to be ____

6. **Our family has traditions.**
    How we are today ____ We need to be ____

7. **Holidays are spent together.**
    How we are today ____ We need to be ____

8. **We eat dinner as a family.**
    How we are today ____ We need to be ____

9. **Vacations are fun times as a family.**
    How we are today ____ We need to be ____

10. **Members are respectful to one another.**
    How we are today ____ We need to be ____

One thing I can begin to do right away to build our family spirituality is _____
_____
_____.

The 24/7 Dad examines his thoughts, feelings and actions on a daily basis to ensure that his actions are respectful to himself, to others, and to his environment. When the 24/7 Dad discovers his actions might have been disrespectful, he apologizes for his actions and is mindful of his future behavior. In order for the 24/7 Dad to do this, he must be "open to change."

Postures towards Acceptance of Change

"Fight or Flight"

This is the posture of defense and attack. When someone suggests change, the person gets into a "fight or flight" mindset.

Some examples of a "Fight or Flight" posture are when someone blames, becomes angry, ignores the need for change, criticizes, starts a fight, or leaves the scene.

"You know Fred, you're never around at night to help put the kids to sleep. I really need your help."

"Well, if you were more organized, you wouldn't need my help. The problem with you is ..."

"Defensive/Closed"

This is the posture of the child. When someone suggests change, the person closes up.

Some examples of a "Defensive/Closed" posture are when someone withdraws, becomes stubborn or silent, denies the need for change, or makes excuses.

"You know Fred, you're never around at night to help put the kids to sleep. I really need your help."

"I don't remember you ever asking me for help. Am I a mind reader?"

"Open for Change"

This is the posture of the 24/7 Dad. When someone suggests change, the person is willing to listen to the need for change.

Some examples of an "Open for Change" posture are when someone makes eye contact (in some cultures, but not in others), looks interested, has a pleasant tone, asks questions, wants to help, and seeks to clarify the needs for change.

"You know Fred, you're never around at night to help put the kids to sleep. I really need your help."

"I'm sorry. I haven't been there to help you. Let's make a plan. What can we do to work together?"

The most important factors in helping you to be "open to change" are:

1. Valuing the need to change. The changes need to have worth before you can make a sincere effort to change.

2. Valuing the other person. If suggestions or observations come from a person who holds little value for you, the comments will seem more like nagging.

3. Be aware of your thoughts and feelings, how you come across to the other person, the mood of the person you are talking with, the situation, etc. You need all of these things so that you can respond in proper ways.

4. Having the appropriate skills and the "know how" to change is an art and a science. Knowing how to change will help create the change.

Weekly Activity Log

Session 5: Spirituality

a. One new thing I learned today was _____
_____
_____
_____

b. The reason this information will help me become a better dad is: _____
_____
_____
_____

Session 6

Physical and Mental Health

On a scale of 1 to 5, with 1 being very low and 5 being very high, I rate how I take care of my physical health _____.

On a scale of 1 to 5, with 1 being very low and 5 being very high, I rate how I take care of my Mental health: _____.

One thing I can do to improve my physical health is _____
_____
_____.

One thing I can do to improve my mental health is _____
_____
_____.

Research over the years has drawn a close relationship between mental health and physical health. The relationship is one of interdependence where one affects the other.

The relationship between mental health and physical health is most aptly demonstrated in the physical response to the feeling of anger.

Stressors are the things in life that cause or contribute to stressful times. Although some of the stressors cannot be controlled, the way we handle our stress can be controlled.

Do women handle their stress differently than men?

Do children have stress? Do babies? What are some of their stressors? How do children handle stress?

Is the parental modeling effect present in the way children handle their stress?

Strategies for Reducing Stress

1. Regular physical exercise
2. Proper diet
3. Regular and sufficient sleep
4. Psychological/marital/spiritual counseling
5. Change jobs or careers
6. Cut back on spending; seek debt consolidation
7. Others:_____

Anger

Anger is often associated with stress, although both can exist independently. Anger is generally a secondary emotion. It is the expression of past pain or hurt. When a feeling is not allowed expression, it is like stepping on a spring. When the pressure is off, feelings spring out. Since all feelings and thoughts have energy, it is the expression of the energy that gets people into trouble.

As young boys, many men have learned that by using fists to hit something (like a pillow) anger is released. Unfortunately, the association of anger and violence has developed into a major social crisis: young boys and men expressing their anger energy into violence.

One way I express my anger is _____
_____
_____.

I learned this expression because _____
_____
_____.

One way my children express their anger is _____
_____
_____.

They learned this way from _____
_____
_____.

How to Express Anger Appropriately

To express anger appropriately, remember the three guidelines:

1. Respect yourself - Don't hurt yourself.
2. Respect others - Don't hurt others.
3. Respect the environment - Don't be disrespectful to your environment.

To express anger appropriately:

Step 1 Find a means of releasing your anger energy appropriately.

Step 2 Talk about what happened.

Sometimes people need to do Step 2 before they do Step 1. The danger here is the volume, tone and content of the message is so full of anger that hurting words are spoken.

Men need to have a plan in place on appropriate ways to express their anger.

Taking Care of Your Health

Some reasons men don't like to go to the doctor are _____
_____
_____
_____.

Men are raised to bury and ignore the physical and mental problems they experience. They're taught that their bodies should be able to "take a licking and keeping on ticking" which leads men to abuse their bodies and ignore warning signs that tell them they need help. What often happens is men ignore the signs for so long that by the time they go to the doctor, it's too late.

FATHERING HANDBOOK • SESSION 6: PHYSICAL AND MENTAL HEALTH

When was the last time you saw the doctor and why? Should the reasons that you've all listed be reasons to keep you from going to the doctor?

Right now the part of my physical or mental health that I am most concerned about is _____

_____

_____

and what I need to do is _____

_____

_____.

Pretend you are your children and write a brief letter to yourself imploring you to take care of your physical and mental health so that you'll be around to see your children graduate, get married, have kids, etc. Be sure to build in some of the things you mentioned you need to do to take better care of yourself.

Three things I need to do to take better care of my **mental** health are:

1. _____
2. _____
3. _____

Three things I need to do to take better care of my **physical** health are:

1. _____
2. _____
3. _____

Weekly Activity Log

Session 6: Physical and Mental Health

a. One new thing I learned today was _____

_____

_____

_____

b. The reason this information will help me become a better dad is: _____

_____

_____

_____

Session 7
Fathering and Family Roles

One memory I have of my father (or father figure) is _____
_____
_____.

What is unique about this memory is _____
_____
_____.

To me, fathering means _____
_____
_____.

To me, mothering means _____
_____
_____.

Fathers have received bad press over the years for their "lack" of some characteristics. Terms like the "Absent Father," the "Abusive Father," and the "Deadbeat Dad" have all painted a bad portrait of dads. Can you think of other negative terms used to describe fathers? _____
_____
_____.

The world clearly has its views of the way fathers "should be." In the following exercise, you will have the chance to create the "Ideal Father."

1. The **Qualities** of an ideal father. What does the ideal father provide to the family?

2. The **Characteristics** of an ideal father. What type of personality and characteristics does the ideal father have?

3. The **Responsibilities** of an ideal father. What responsibilities does the ideal father take on in his role?

"The Ideal Father"

1. **Qualities** of the Ideal Father. The ideal father provides the following to his family:

a. _____
b. _____
c. _____
d. _____
e. _____
f. _____

FATHERING HANDBOOK • SESSION 7: FATHERING AND FAMILY ROLES

2. **Characteristics** of the Ideal Father. The ideal father has the following personality and characteristics:

a. _____
b. _____
c. _____
d. _____
e. _____
f. _____

3. **Responsibilities** of an Ideal Father. An ideal father takes on the following responsibilities:

a. _____
b. _____
c. _____
d. _____
e. _____
f. _____

Being a father and being a partner are roles men take on in their family. Family roles have different responsibilities. It's the way and style in which men carry out their responsibilities that can make the difference in a happy, healthy family, or in a troubled, unhappy family.

Being a caring and loving father and partner is linked to being a caring and loving man. The qualities of who we are as men are the same qualities we express in our family roles. The 24/7 Dad expresses these traits as a father and partner. An uncaring man expresses these traits as an uncaring father and partner. The 24/7 Dad is a caring man expressed in all aspects of daily life.

Father/Partner Checklist

Place a **Y** (Yes), **N** (No) or **S** (Sometimes) on the line by the characteristics you feel best represent the type of father and partner you are. If you are not currently in a relationship as a husband or partner, rate yourself as you believe you could be in future relationships.

Y = Yes, this is me.
N = No, this is not me.
S = Sometimes this is me.

1. **I am open to listening to other points of view.**
   Father _____ Partner _____
2. **I can negotiate and compromise.**
   Father _____ Partner _____
3. **I am clearly in charge.**
   Father _____ Partner _____
4. **I expect others to follow the rules I set down.**
   Father _____ Partner _____
5. **I demand respect.**
   Father _____ Partner _____
6. **I appropriately communicate how I feel.**
   Father _____ Partner _____
7. **I am willing to change my ideas.**
   Father _____ Partner _____
8. **I express a sense of closeness to those I love.**
   Father _____ Partner _____
9. **I like being in control.**
   Father _____ Partner _____
10. **I enjoy spending quality time with my family.**
    Father _____ Partner _____
11. **I am able to listen to the good as well as the bad.**
    Father _____ Partner _____
12. **I am clearly seen as a friend.**
    Father _____ Partner _____
13. **Others can come to me to talk.**
    Father _____ Partner _____
14. **I am caring and giving.**
    Father _____ Partner _____
15. **I easily have fun.**
    Father _____ Partner _____

7 Benefits of Marriage

1. Healthy Children
Children who grow up in a home with their two married parents are healthier, on average, than are children who grow up in a home in which their parents just live together. Children who grow up with their married parents are, for example, less likely to be abused and to misbehave in or drop out of school. These children are more likely to have good marriages of their own and to not wind up as a pregnant teen or to abuse alcohol or drugs. Marriage gives children the best chance at a healthy life!

2. Healthy Marriages Lead to Strong Relationships with Children
Marriage provides the best chance for fathers to create strong relationships with their children. Men who wait to have kids until they marry are three times more likely to be involved in their children's lives than are men who have kids outside of marriage. Dads who have good marriages are, on average, more involved in their children's lives than are never-married or divorced dads. That's because it's easier for married men to be with their children every day, and to nurture their kids at every stage of growth. Marriage can provide the joy of growing with your children every day!

3. Better Family Finances
Married couples have twice the money and assets that unmarried couples do. This can create a better financial future for couples and their children. And married men are more likely to save and invest, even when they have the same income as unmarried men. Marriage also comes with tax, inheritance and Social Security benefits. Marriage can help you make the most of your family's finances!

4. Fuller, Happier Lives
Married men are more likely to say they are happy than are unmarried men. After divorce, men are worse off overall than are women. The well-being of the family is the highest priority for most married men. When men focus on their wives and their children, not just on themselves, it helps them to lead full, happy lives. And married men are less likely to be depressed. Marriage gives men more family members they can turn to for social, emotional and financial support. Marriage can benefit you through a focus on the family!

5. A Long, Healthy Life
A full, happy life often leads to a long, healthy life. On average, married men live longer than do unmarried men. Married men are more likely to take care of themselves. For example, they're more likely to stay in shape and to get medical help when they need it. And married men are less likely to do things that can hurt them, such as smoking, drinking, or using illegal drugs. Marriage can give you a great chance at a long, healthy life!

6. More, Better, and Safer Sex
One sign of a full, happy life is an active, good, and safe sex life. Married couples say they have sex more often than do unmarried people. And married men say they have better sex than do unmarried men. Married men work hard to build healthy relationships with their wives. They know that sex is best when they stay faithful to one woman. They also know that sex is best when they are emotionally close to their wives. And when a husband and a wife are faithful, sex is safer physically and emotionally. There is little chance that you will get a sexual disease if you and your wife are faithful. Marriage can give you the best chance for an active, great, and safe sex life!

7. Increased Faithfulness
One reason that sex is better and safer in marriage is that married men and women are, on average, more faithful to each other than are men and women who simply live together or who date. You may be surprised to learn that most married men and women are faithful to each other. One study found that only 4 percent of wives are unfaithful compared to 20 percent of unmarried women who live with a man and 18 percent of women who date. Marriage can reduce the chance that the woman you love will cheat on you!

Adapted from The 7 Benefits of Marriage For Men Brochure published by National Fatherhood Initiative℠ ©2004

Weekly Activity Log

Session 7: Fathering and Family Roles

a. One new thing I learned today was _____
_____
_____
_____.

b. The reason this information will help me become a better dad is: _____
_____
_____
_____
_____.

Session 8
Fathering and Culture

One tradition my Dad (parents) passed on to me that I would like to pass down to my children is

_____
_____
_____
_____.

The reason I would like to pass this tradition on is

_____
_____
_____
_____.

Culture is a set of rules, beliefs, values and norms that guide a specific group of people at a specific point in time. Some examples of cultural groups are:

- Race (Black, White, Latino, Asian, etc.)
- Country of Origin (France, USA, Bolivia, etc.)
- Ethnicity (German, African, Chinese, etc)
- Religion (Baptist, Catholic, Methodist, etc.)
- Job and Careers (lawyer, carpenter, etc.)
- Gender (male or female)
- Age (youth, adolescent, adult, elder)
- Political (liberal, conservative, etc.)
- Income (rich, poor, welfare, etc.)
- Education (high school, college, etc)
- Sports (golfers, swimmers, etc)
- Music (rock, rap, etc)
- Art (film, media, etc.)

Some examples of "counter-cultures" would be:
- Drug users
- Tax evaders
- Terrorists
- Gangs

Why do people choose to be "counter culture?"

Morals are the "rights and wrongs" of behaviors experienced by an individual, family, culture or government. Morals are the "rights and wrongs" we learned as children.

One moral I learned in childhood that I still practice today is _____
_____.

because _____
_____.

One moral I learned in childhood that I don't practice today is _____
because_____
_____.

One moral I teach my children that they practice is _____
because_____
_____.

One moral I teach my children that they don't practice is_____
because_____
_____.

The "whys" to the morals that men and children practice or don't practice are directly related to values. (In other words, "why" you do something is related to what is important to you.)

A **value** is something that has worth. Values as they relate to beliefs and behaviors are morals that have worth.

For morals and values to mean something, men must **model** morals and values, or "walk the talk." Modeling is a vital teacher of morals and values. Dads who say one thing but do another don't "walk the talk." Instead, they confuse children. The result is an example of a moral that has no positive value.

The model of not "walking the talk" or "do as I say and not as I do" does teach children a moral—a negative one.

- When men don't do as they say, what are the children learning?
- What is the moral lesson the fathers are teaching?

The bottom line is that children learn the "value" of not following through on commitments, on being disrespectful, and being irresponsible.

Cultural Values and Traditions

Family Cultural Inventory

Complete the inventory by responding to each statement.

1. List three cultural **values/traditions** that you are passing on to your children. Describe what you do that models the value or tradition.

Cultural Value/Tradition: _____
_____.

The way I model this value/tradition is: _____
_____.

Cultural Value/Tradition: _____
_____.

The way I model this value/tradition is: _____
_____.

Cultural Value/Tradition: _____
_____.

The way I model this value/tradition is: _____
_____.

2. List three cultural **practices/beliefs** you would like to pass on to your children but aren't doing a very good job with:

Cultural Practice/Belief:_____
_____.

The actions I need to take to pass this practice/belief on are: _____
_____.

Cultural Practice/Belief:_____
_____.

The actions I need to take to pass this practice/belief on are:_____
_____.

Cultural Practice/Belief: _____
_____.

The actions I need to take to pass this practice/belief on _____
_____.

FATHERING HANDBOOK • **SESSION 8: FATHERING AND CULTURE**

Weekly Activity Log

Session 8: Fathering and Culture

a. One new thing I learned today was _____
_____
_____
_____
_____.

b. The reason this information will help me become a better dad is: _____
_____
_____
_____
_____.

Notes

Session 9
Discipline, Rewards and Punishment

One memory I have of being "disciplined" by my father (parents) is _____
_____
_____
_____
_____.

What I learned from this experience was _____
_____
_____
_____
_____.

Discipline

Discipline comes from a Latin word "discipulus" meaning "to teach; to guide." The follower of a teacher is called a "disciple." A disciple believes in the morals, values and behaviors of the teacher. A disciple practices what was taught by his or her teacher.

A father is a teacher—one who guides his children. Children are the disciples of their father. The father is a teacher of morals and values.

There are different types of teachers with different styles of teaching. It is important to remember that children learn two ways: from the **direct experiences** they have with their teacher, and from the **observations** they have of their teacher's behavior.

Use the list below and pick out your style of discipline.

- Authoritarian
- Strict
- Dictator
- Permissive
- Wishy-washy
- Democratic
- King of the House
- Ruler
- Uninvolved
- Controlling
- Punitive
- Nurturing
- Easy
- Shaming
- Fair
- Other: _____

My style of teaching discipline to my children would be called _____
_____
_____
_____.

My father's style of teaching discipline to me was
_____
_____
_____
_____.

In the box on the next page, take about 5 minutes to draw your style of discipline from your children's point of view. That is, how do you think your children see your style of discipline?

You can draw faces, designs, pictures, etc.

My Discipline (From My Children's Point of View)

For discipline to be a good for you and your children, three factors are vital:

- Negative styles that say your children are "no good" or "bad" are very harmful. When dads use shaming, guilt, cruel words, or blame, children don't learn that what they did is not okay, they learn that they are not okay.

- Discipline must focus on the "action" not on the "actor." Any type of physical punishment says to children that they are a "bad person," and takes the focus away from the action.

- After you have disciplined or punished your children, you must restore your relationship with them by saying that you still love them no matter what (you love them "unconditionally").

With my style of discipline, I want to make sure my children learn _____
_____
_____.

What I'm afraid they might be learning is _____
_____
_____.

Sometimes what we intend to teach is not always what children learn.

Family Rules

Many men feel that discipline means "to control" rather than "to teach or to guide." As a result, some dads use fear to punish their children. Examples include: threats of the loss of love, safety, belonging, privileges, etc.

To be successful, discipline needs to be clear, consistent
and doable. To achieve this goal, you must establish Family Rules. The purpose of **Family Rules** is to ensure that children succeed in discipline.

Steps in Establishing Family Rules

1. Call a family meeting.

2. Mention that all family members are going to help establish the Family Rules.

3. Divide a large sheet of paper (poster board) into halves by drawing a line down the middle.

4. Label one side **Do's** and the other side **Don'ts**. For every **Don't**, there needs to be a **Do**, otherwise children are learning only **Don'ts**.

5. Get the rules from the children. Ask, "What kind of rule should we have about ____?" Issues might be homework, hanging up clothes, calling home when you're going to be late, etc.

6. Come up with a **Do** (Do homework before dinner.) and a **Don't** (Don't wait until after supper to do your homework.).

7. Keep the entire list to around 5 to 7 rules. Too many rules can confuse children.

Every rule needs a consequence so that children learn the basic idea of discipline. A simple formula is "If-Then" as in, "If you do _____, then _____ will happen." The If-Then formula helps children learn to make good choices.

The purpose of punishment is to provide a negative consequence to an inappropriate behavior so that children will learn to replace that behavior with an appropriate one.

Rewards and Punishments

For your children to learn appropriate behaviors, you need to reward them. Rewards are positive consequences given for appropriate behaviors that create the value in your children to behave appropriately.

There are five types of Rewards and Punishments that help children learn right from wrong (morals). These are not punishments like slapping, yelling or bribing children that teach children that they—not their behavior—are bad. These five positive consequences (Rewards) and negative consequences (Punishments) also help you teach your children the value of treating others with respect.

Rewards

Praise
Compliment your children for behaving properly (what they do) and compliment them with love (who they are)

Gentle Touch
Give your children hugs, massages, pats, high fives, etc.

Privileges
Allow your children to stay up later, have extra story time, etc.

Objects
Give your children toys, stickers, etc.

Allowance
To help children ten years and older manage their money. Give an allowance for chores done.

Punishments

Being Grounded
Children can't leave the house because they left the house without asking or they broke curfew.

Time-Out
A brief period of inactivity to a chair in an area away from others for a serious breaking of the Family Rules, morals or values.

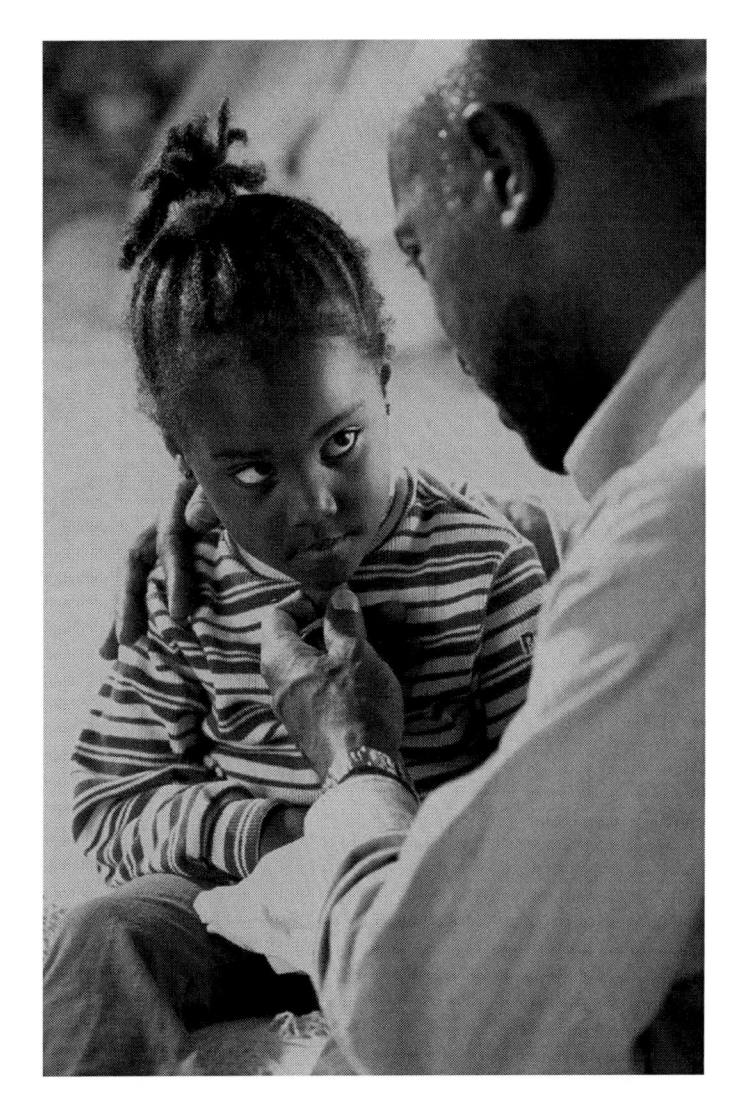

Loss of Privilege
Children lose a privilege when they misuse an object or privilege on purpose.

Restitution ("Paying Back")
Children must clean up a mess, replace an object broken on purpose, perform in-home community service (such as cleaning a fish tank, raking leaves, or vacuuming), etc.

Parental Disappointment
You tell your children how disappointed you are for a bad decision or action done on purpose.

Weekly Activity Log

Session 9: Discipline, Rewards and Punishment

a. One new thing I learned today was _____

_____

_____

_____

_____

b. The reason this information will help me become a better dad is: _____

_____

_____

_____

_____

Notes

Session 10
Expectations and Children's Development

One childhood expectation my parents had for me that I was **able** to achieve was _____

_____

and when I did this, I felt _____

_____.

One childhood expectation my parents had for me that I was **unable** to achieve was _____

_____

and when I did not do this, I felt _____

_____.

Self-Worth is the overall value a person has for himself. Self-worth is a person's self-concept (thoughts about himself) and self-esteem (feelings about himself) combined.

An overall self-worth is pretty solid over time. Still, a self-concept or self-esteem may move between positive or negative (or high or low) depending upon an event in a person's life.

Parental Expectations are the behavior and abilities that parents expect from their children.

When expectations can't be met, what is likely to happen to the child's self-worth?

When expectations are met, what is likely to happen to a child's self-worth?

Nature
The characteristics a person is born with (height, race, color of hair, learning abilities, special learning needs, gender, DNA, etc).

Nurture
The way a person is raised as a child and treated throughout life that affects how his personality develops.

Nature vs. Nurture
Do people turn out to be the way they are because of nature or because of nurture?

People have asked the nature vs. nurture question for hundreds of years. Today, it's known that people are the way they are as a result of both nature and nurture acting as one. The way parents and culture raise children can strengthen a natural characteristic or weaken it. Parents and culture can support or hold back children's talents. Talents "shine" when they are nurtured and weaken when they are neglected or punished.

Much the same holds true with children's abilities at different stages of development. As with any structure, the foundation of a child's development is very important. Parents who know how to get their children off to a good start increase the chance of their children growing into healthy, caring and nurturing individuals.

AGES & STAGES
(See Appendix)

There are two key points to know about the "Ages & Stages" information listed in the Appendix:

1. These charts may worry some parents. Don't let the charts frighten you. They can be helpful. The fact is that there is too much information on child development to know it all without looking to the charts for help. Even pediatricians (doctors for children) keep these charts to refer to in their work!

2. Don't use these charts like report cards. Don't use them to compare your children to other children or to each other. They are only road maps to guide you toward the abilities that children should have at a certain age. All children develop differently. The most vital thing is that your children acquire these abilities eventually. If you are ever worried about how your child is developing, talk with your child's doctor.

Weekly Activity Log

Session 10: Expectations and Children's Development

a. One new thing I learned today was _____

_____

_____

_____

b. The reason this information will help me become a better dad is: _____

_____

_____

_____

_____

Session 11
Balancing Work and Family

The role model my father gave me on balancing work and family was _____
_____
_____
_____.

What I learned from this model was _____
_____
_____
_____.

One thing I would like to do differently is _____
_____
_____
_____.

Work and Family Questionnaire

1. Three pleasures I get from my **work** are: ____
_____
_____
_____.

2. Three pleasures I get from being with my **family** are: _____
_____
_____
_____.

3. To me, my **job** means: _____
_____
_____
_____.

4. To me, my **family** means: _____
_____
_____
_____.

5. The greatest benefit I get from my **job** that I don't get from being with my family is: _____
_____
_____
_____.

6. The greatest benefit I get from my **family** that I don't get from my job is: _____

_____

_____

_____

_____.

7. The degree of joy I get from being at work is (circle one):

    1   2   3   4   5

  A little   Average   A lot

8. The degree of joy I get from being with my family is (circle one):

    1   2   3   4   5

  A little   Average   A lot

9. The percentage of my time at home that I spend with my family during the week is ____ %.

10. The percentage of my time at home that I spend on my work during the week is ____ %.

11. Typically, I leave for work at _____ and return home at _____.

My current employment is a (check one)
- Job _____
- Career _____
- Work _____

What do you think makes employment a job, career, or work?

Male vs. Female Work Roles

Please respond to this list by indicating if you feel the job or career is better suited for females (F), males (M), or both (B).

Job	
Hairdresser	_____
House Painter	_____
Window washer	_____
Professional Basketball Player	_____
Cab Driver	_____
Teacher	_____
Flight Attendant	_____
Soldier	_____
Maid	_____
Referee	_____
Bell Hop	_____
Minister	_____
Sales Clerk	_____
Banker	_____
CEO	_____
Farmer	_____
Professional Soccer Player	_____
Airline Pilot	_____
Singer	_____
Parent	_____
Musician	_____
Construction Worker	_____
Receptionist	_____
Secretary	_____
Nurse	_____
Doctor	_____
Dentist	_____
Day Care Worker	_____
Chef	_____
Waiter	_____
Sanitation Worker	_____

Are some jobs labeled strictly as male or female?

Are some jobs and careers better suited for one gender than another?

The expectation I have for my **son** is that he should have a (check one)
    ___ Career ___ Job.

The career or job should be _____
_____.

The expectation I have for my **daughter** is that she should have a (check one)
    ___ Career ___ Job.

The career or job should be _____
_____.

Are the expectations you have for your sons different than the expectations you have for your daughters?

Are they different based only on gender?
Are the expectations you have of your children related
to things you haven't achieved in your own life?

One thing I want for my children related to balancing work and family that I haven't been able to accomplish is _____
_____
_____
_____
_____.

Things that keep me from balancing work and family are _____
_____
_____
_____
_____.

Creating a Father-Friendly Workplace

1. Allow Your Employees Time Off to Be Good Dads
An increasing number of men report lost productivity due to family concerns. Implementing a workplace policy that encourages fathers to take time off for the birth or adoption of a child is an appreciated benefit and can help to increase productivity. Also, allowing fathers a reasonable number of opportunities to attend special family events, such as a school play or sporting event, and to fulfill family obligations, such as taking a child to a doctor's appointment, can help to foster invaluable loyalty to an organization.

2. Implement a "Take Your Child to Work Day"
Young children are often curious about where daddy goes all day and what he does. One way to satisfy this curiosity and build good relationships with children is to allow fathers to take their children to work. Some organizations have taken this idea a step further, and have created workplace day-care centers. This provides the parents an opportunity to visit with their children during breaks and over lunch.

3. Establish Flexible Spending Accounts
As working families face greater economic pressures, one way to ease these burdens is to allow employees to shelter some of their income from taxation for specific purposes such as medical and child care expenses. Implementing a flexible spending account can help alleviate these financial burdens by increasing the amount of disposable income a family can allocate to child care and family expenses.

4. Allow Flex-time and Flexible Work Hours
Although the ability of employers to implement flex-time policies will vary due in part to state and federal laws governing employment, in general, flex-time allows an employee to exchange overtime hours for days off. Rather than being paid time and a half, an employee would be allowed to

schedule time with his family without fear of losing income. In addition, flexible work arrangements permit employees to schedule their work day to ensure they also have time to fulfill their family obligations.

5. Encourage Tele-commuting

This policy allows employees to work at home both full and part-time by maintaining an electronic connection to the office via e-mail, fax, and telephone. In addition, tele-commuting employees have the potential to out-perform their counterparts in the office by not having to deal with "office distractions." This policy also allows many parents the added benefit of home care for non-infant children, while relieving stress of commutes. To maintain a high level of productivity for tele-commuters, it is important for employers to offer plenty of management and technical support in addition to stressing results and output.

6. Initiate Fatherhood Education Seminars in the Workplace

Employers often allow their employees to take work-related seminars on topics ranging from enhancing computer skills to organizing one's personal life. A fatherhood education seminar could easily be added to an employer's seminar program. Several organizations offer workplace-based fatherhood skills training and the National Fatherhood Initiative provides a listing of organizations that offer this type of training.

7. Set Up Leave Banks

This allows employees with excessive vacation or personal days to donate their extra time to employees who may need additional time to fulfill family obligations and commitments.

8. Permit Shift Swapping

Shift swapping allows employees the flexibility to exchange their work shifts with other employees so that they can take a child to the doctor, attend a child's sporting event, or meet other family obligations.

9. Encourage Job Sharing

Job sharing allows two part-time employees to share the tasks of one full-time position. This allows parent-employees greater flexibility in balancing work and family responsibilities. Job sharing also provides the employer with a less expensive alternative to a full-time employee with benefits.

10. Provide Comprehensive Health Benefits Programs

One of the major concerns of parents today is providing good health care for their children. By enabling employees access to comprehensive health benefits such as health and vision care, mental health services and dental coverage, employees will be able to provide the necessary health and medical care needed for growing children.

Adapted from the Creating a Father-Friendly Workplace Brochure published by National Fatherhood Initiative℠ ©2001

Weekly Activity Log

Session 11: Balancing Work and Family

a. One new thing I learned today was _____

_____

_____

_____

_____

b. The reason this information will help me become a better dad is: _____

_____

_____

_____

_____

Notes

FATHERING HANDBOOK • SESSION 12: GETTING INVOLVED WITH YOUR CHILDREN

Session 12
Getting Involved with Your Children

When I recall my childhood, one way my dad (parents) was involved in my life was _____
_____
_____
_____
_____ .

One way I wish my dad (parents) had been more involved was _____
_____
_____
_____
_____ .

One way that I am involved in my children's lives is _____
_____
_____
_____
_____ .

What this means to me is _____
_____
and what it means to my children is _____
_____
_____
_____
_____ .

"Ways Dads Can Be Involved Checklist"

Please check off the box that best describes your involvement with your children.

1. Being a daily parent

   ____ ____ ____ ____
   None Little Often A Lot

2. Attending parent-teacher conferences

   ____ ____ ____ ____
   None Little Often A Lot

3. Attending performances (dance, sports, etc.)

   ____ ____ ____ ____
   None Little Often A Lot

4. Reading stories to children

   ____ ____ ____ ____
   None Little Often A Lot

5. Helping children with homework

   ____ ____ ____ ____
   None Little Often A Lot

6. Preparing meals

   ____ ____ ____ ____
   None Little Often A Lot

7. Doing outdoor projects with your children

   ____ ____ ____ ____
   None Little Often A Lot

8. Gardening with your children

   ____ ____ ____ ____
   None Little Often A Lot

9. Bedtime stories and tucking your children in

   ____ ____ ____ ____
   None Little Often A Lot

10. Diapering and dressing your children

   ____ ____ ____ ____
   None Little Often A Lot

11. Playing games with your children

   ____ ____ ____ ____
   None Little Often A Lot

12. Taking your kids to work for a day

   ____ ____ ____ ____
   None Little Often A Lot

13. Meeting/knowing your children's friends and their parents

   ____ ____ ____ ____
   None Little Often A Lot

14. Talking with your children about their interests

   ____ ____ ____ ____
   None Little Often A Lot

15. Asking your children how their day went

   ____ ____ ____ ____
   None Little Often A Lot

How to Help Your Child Do Well in School

1. Don't Let Mom Do All the Work
Some dads leave everything to do with school up to mom. This includes helping with school work, meetings with teachers and volunteering for school and class events. When you are not involved, it gives your child only one parent to help. If you're married to mom, helping with school work, meetings and events gives mom a break. Getting involved will help your child and your marriage. It takes the pressure off mom and shows your wife and your child that you respect her.

2. "Show and Tell" How Important School Is
Your child needs to hear you say that school is important to success in life. Tell your child that the better he or she does in school, the better chance your child will have at getting a job that he or she will like and that pays well. Take the time to talk with your child every day about the school day.

Model how important school is by taking a course on something you want to learn. If your child is old enough, take your child to class with you. This will show that learning can be done at any age. Buy books for your child or take your child to the library. Let your child choose the books to read. If you have a computer, buy software that teaches your child about math, reading, writing and other subjects. Make sure the software is designed for your child's age.

3. Help with School Work
Children today have more school work, or homework, than you may have had as a child. This puts a lot of pressure on children and the parents who help them.

Helping with school work may help your child learn more. You may be better at some subjects than mom is. She may be better at other subjects than you are. Your child may be in a class of 20 to 30 students. If your child is having problems, your child may not get as much one-on-one help as he or she needs. You and mom can give your child the kind of one-on-one help the school may not be able to give.

If you have a boy, you may need to focus on reading and writing. If you have a girl, you may need to focus on math. Boys tend to do better in math than girls do, and girls tend to do better in reading and writing. (This may not be true of your boy or girl.) Look for your child's strength and weaknesses, so that you can help your child where he or she needs it most.

Adapted from How To Help Your Child In School published by National Fatherhood Initiative℠ ©2003

4. Make School Fun
Your child should have fun learning no matter how old he or she is. Play games that teach basic skills to your child, like math, reading and writing. Use the fun times you spend with your child as a chance to learn. If you and your child like to fish, for example, go over school work that your child has problems with while you wait to catch the big one. If you're watching a basketball game, ask your child by how many points the winning team is ahead.

Encourage your child to play sports, join school clubs, play in the school band or get involved in student government. This will not only make school fun, it will help your child do better in school and stay out of trouble.

5. Spend a Day or Two in Class
Ask your child's teachers if you can spend parts of one or two days in the classroom. This will give you an idea not only of the subjects your child learns, but how the teacher teaches them. It helps to know how the teacher teaches math, reading, writing and other subjects. It may be different from the way you learned those things. You don't want to confuse your child by being taught one way at school and another way at home.

6. Go to School and Class Events
Go to meetings with the teacher, to class parties, to school ball games and plays, and to events that involve the entire school. When dads do these things, their children get better grades and like school more.

7. Meet with the Teacher
Set a time to meet with your child's teacher before you spend a day or two in class. This will help you get to know the teacher and ask questions you may have about how the teacher will teach and discipline your child. Offer to help with class events or to help (tutor) students in subjects you know well. Meet with the teacher as often as you need to. The teacher won't mind because it will show that you want to be involved. It's also good to meet with the principal to see how the school is run.

8. Join a Group That Helps Parents to Become Involved
Become a member of a group, like the PTA, that helps parents to get involved in your child's school. This is one of the best ways to make sure that your child's teacher is doing the best he or she can to teach your child. Start a "Dad's Club" as part of the group. The club can create projects and events that help dads to get involved in the school.

9. Get to Know Other Children and Parents
Your child will make friends in class and may or may not get along with others. Knowing the children in the class, and their parents, will help you talk with your child about the good and not so good things that happen at school. This will help if you need to talk with the teacher about problems between your child and other children that happen over and over again. Invite the children and the parents that you want your child to be around to your home. This may create bonds that last a long time. One of the best things you can do for your child is to help him or her avoid "hanging out" with the wrong crowd.

10. Ask Your Boss for Time Off
All these ideas may be great, but what if it's hard to get off work? Use benefits, like flextime, that will allow you to get involved. Go in a little late and stay a little late if your child has an event in the morning. Bring your work home and do it after your child goes to bed if it will help you arrange your day to get involved. Ask the teacher or school for a calendar of events so that you can ask for time off long before events take place. This will help your boss plan for your absence. Ask to "telecommute" so that you can take and pick up your child from school.

Weekly Activity Log

Session 12: Getting Involved With Your Children

a. One new thing I learned today was _____
_____
_____
_____
_____

b. The reason this information will help me become a better dad is: _____
_____
_____
_____
_____

"Resolving Differences of Opinion"

1. Understand the origin of your point of view. Where did it come from? What is it related to?

2. Understand the opposite point of view, not from your viewpoint, but from the other person's viewpoint.

3. Ask yourself the following: "Why do I need to defend my point of view? What am I holding on to?"

4. Develop a sense of openness. Keep yourself open to hearing the other person.

5. Recognize that the point of view of the other person is as important to him/her as yours is to you.

6. Attempt to understand the other person from "inside his/her shoes."

7. See the other person as having value (importance or worth). Otherwise, it will be next to impossible to value what they believe in. You can value the other person but disagree with their point of view.

8. Compromise (give and take). What can each of you give to the other? What is each of you willing to let go of?

9. Establish rules for discussion.
    - Set a time limit of 15 to 30 minutes.
    - No attacking the other person's character/personality.
    - No name calling
    - Stick to the subject.
    - Use the past only as it pertains to the present.
    - Keep calm.
    - Be respectful to each other.

10. Recognize it might take several times to talk about the issue to resolve it.

Notes

Notes

Appendix:
Ages & Stages

# First and Second Months

Physical Development	Motor Skills	Adaptive Development	Social Development
Average weight gain of about 5 to 7 ounces each week for the first 6 months. Height gain of approx. one inch each month Primarily breaths through nose	Typically unable to hold head up in first month, can turn head from side to side when lying on back, by second month will lift head. If held in a standing position, body will be limp at knees and hips. In supported position, back is rounded by second month, will try to hold head up but it will still bob forward. In first month, hands will usually be closed with grasp reflex strong, by second month hands frequently open and grasp, reflex fades.	Can fix eyes on moving object when held at a distance of 8–15 inches, by two months will follow toy from side to side. Prefers responsive human faces. Will quiet when hears your voice by two months, recognizes familiar voices. First month cries to show discomfort / distress.	Watches parent's face intently as he / she smiles at or plays with infant.

Parental Support and Encouragement

1. Holding, cuddling, rocking, talking and singing to your baby increases his (and your) sense of security.
2. Know that as you console and comfort your infant, he may not always be consolable regardless of what you do.
3. If your time together is limited, playing, talking and singing during his alert stages (dressing, bathing, feeding, walking, driving) is more fun for you both.
4. Start to establish bathing/feeding/bedtime routines and other habits to encourage predictable care patterns and discourage night awakening.
5. Stimulate your child by using age appropriate toys in your play interactions.
6. Discuss your questions about your baby's health and temperament with your healthcare professional, including how you are doing/feeling as this particular baby's father.

With contributions from Dr. Kyle Pruett, Yale University

Third and Fourth Months

Physical Development	Motor Skills	Adaptive Development	Social Development
Increasing control of physical movements in neck, arms, legs and trunk. Soft spot on crown of head still open. (Careful!) Drooling begins.	Holds head more erect, more often. Can sit erect if propped up. Able to raise head and chest up, bears weight on forearms. Will briefly support some weight on legs if stood up. Inspects and plays with own hands. Can grasp and hold a rattle. Can bring objects to his mouth. (Careful!) Will clutch at blankets or clothes.	Locates sound by turning head and looking in same direction. Beginning hand-eye coordination. Starts to cry less often and cause is easier to discern. "Talks" a great deal when spoken to. Laughs, squeals, babbles, chuckles, and coos to show pleasure/excitement. Plays patty cake and peek-a-boo games.	Social smile begins to appear. Enjoy! Displays considerable interest in surroundings. Recognizes familiar faces and objects and shows pleasure. Seeks attention by vocalizing/moving/fussing, ceases to cry when familiar face enters the room. Begins to show memory of routines. Will turn away from over-stimulation and over-excitement

Parental Support and Encouragement

1. Continue to nurture your baby by holding, cuddling, rocking, etc.
2. Encourage baby's vocalization by talking and singing to him, mimicking the sounds he contributes to the "conversation".
3. Read and play simple games with your baby.
4. Help your baby learn self-consoling techniques by providing him with the same comfort object at bedtime or in new situations. He/she'll eventually choose one (blanket, stuffed animal, etc.). This encourages independence over time, not dependence.
5. Establish a bedtime routine and encourage your baby to console himself by putting him to bed awake after you have helped him quiet down.
6. Encourage play with age appropriate toys.

With contributions from Dr. Kyle Pruett, Yale University

Fifth and Sixth Months

Physical Development	Motor Skills	Adaptive Development	Social Development
Birth weight has doubled. Growth rate slows. Baby may only gain 3 to 5 oz. and grow 1/2 inch each month for the next 6 months. Brain tissue still growing fast, but still fragile (still no shaking or roughhousing). Starts to get lower center teeth.	Able to sit for longer periods when back is well supported. Can bear most of weight when held (briefly) in standing position. Can roll from stomach to back. (Careful!) Puts feet to mouth. Sits in a high chair with back straight. Can grasp objects voluntarily. Takes objects directly to mouth. Holds bottle with both hands (briefly).	Looks for a dropped object, may initiate game. Able to sustain prolonged visual inspection of an object. Will turn head to side, and then look up or down. Squeals and coos in delight or excitement.	Smiles at own mirror image. Pats bottle or breast with both hands. Initiates more play. Holds up both arms to be picked up. Vocalizes displeasure when object/familiar person is taken away. Imitates (cough, tongue noises, etc.). Has frequent emotion changes.

Parental Support and Encouragement

1. Encourage your baby to talk by copying sounds she/he enjoys making.
2. Read to your baby and play music (of all kinds).
3. Play social games (patty cake, peek-a-boo, hide and seek with people/objects).
4. Establish limits on behavior (throwing) at this age, using distraction, stimulus control, structure and routine. Too early to establish discipline.
5. Keep up bathing/feeding/bedtime routine and other habits to discourage fatigue, disorganization and night awakening.
6. Encourage the baby to learn to console him/herself by putting him or her to bed awake.

With contributions from Dr. Kyle Pruett, Yale University

Seventh and Eighth Months

Physical Development	Motor Skills	Adaptive Development	Social Development
Develops upper central teeth. Begins to show pattern in emptying bladder and bowel movements.	Sits, leaning forward on both hands. Bears full weight on feet in standing position, bounces actively. Transfers objects from one hand to the other. Bangs objects together. Rakes with fingers at small objects. Begins pinching grasp with fingers of smaller objects. Releases object at will (or not). Reaches for toys out of reach.	Responds to own name. Localizes sound by turning head and attending. Has beginning taste preferences. Produces vowel sounds and chain syllables (baba, dada, kiki) but does not know their meaning. Utterances, signal emphasis, preferences and emotion.	Is aware of non-family/familiar adults and increasingly aware of and possibly fearful of strangers. Imitates simple acts and noises. Can attract attention by coughing or snorting. Demonstrates dislike of food by keeping lips closed. Can exhibit aggressiveness/excitement by biting. Looks briefly for toy that disappears. Beginning response to word "no".

Parental Support and Encouragement

1. Encourage your baby to talk by talking to him, incorporating his new sounds in the "conversation".
2. Increase baby's social circle and involve baby in your social activities, with an eye on not too many strange handlers at once.
3. Read and sing to your baby and play music (of all kinds).
4. Play games (patty cake, peek-a-boo, tickle bee, etc).
5. Provide age appropriate toys.
6. Keep small objects out of reach.
7. To set limits for the infant at this age, use distraction, monitor stimulus amounts, structure, and routine.
8. Limit the number of rules but consistently enforce them.
9. Maintain the bedtime routine. Encourage the baby to learn to console him/herself by putting him/her to bed awake.

With contributions from Dr. Kyle Pruett, Yale University

Ninth and Tenth Months

Physical Development	Motor Skills	Adaptive Development	Social Development
More teeth erupt. (Distressing) Infant is able to raise head while lying down or in a sitting position.	Starts to crawl, may progress backward at first, by 10th month will be pulling self forward. (Careful!) Can change from lying position to sitting position. Sits steadily on floor for longer periods. Pulls up and stands holding onto furniture. Uses thumb and index finger in crude pincher grasp of small objects. Dominant hand use can start to appear.	Depth perception is increasing. Turns head directly toward sound. Responds to simple commands. Says "dada" and "mama" with beginning meaning. Imitates definite speech sounds. Speaks gibberish (sounds like a sentence but isn't yet).	Parents increasingly important as play and comfort partners. Increased interest in pleasing parent. May show fear of going to bed or being left alone. Puts arm in front of face to avoid washing. Imitates expressions. Likes attention; will repeat action or pull at your clothes to attract attention. Cries when scolded/scared. Demonstrates beginning independence in dressing, feeding and testing parents.

Parental Support and Encouragement

1. Your baby is in motion, so make sure your home is baby proof to prevent unnecessary accidents.
2. Provide an area where baby can explore and practice new skills.
3. Talk with your baby, respond to his/her vocal efforts.
4. Read to and sing to your baby and play music (of all kinds).
5. Play social games (patty cake, peek-a-boo, etc.).
6. Provide age appropriate toys.
7. To set limits on physical aggression and discipline with the infant at this age, use distraction, monitor stimulus load, structure, and routine.
8. Limit the number of rules but consistently enforce them.
9. Maintain an established bedtime routine.

With contributions from Dr. Kyle Pruett, Yale University

Eleventh and Twelfth Months

Physical Development	Motor Skills	Adaptive Development	Social Development
More teeth grow in. Birth weight has probably tripled and height has doubled since birth. Soft spot on head is almost closed.	Crawls well. Walks holding onto furniture or your hand. Can sit down from standing position. When sitting, pivots to reach toward back to pick up an object. Holds a crayon. Explores objects more thoroughly. (Still uses mouth—careful!) Drops objects into a container (any container). Can turn pages in a book, usually many at a time	Can follow rapidly moving objects. Comprehends hundreds of words although toddlers may only speak two or three words. Recognizes objects by name. Understands simple one stage commands.	Experiences joy/esteem when a task is mastered. Reacts to restrictions with frustration. Shows emotions of all kinds. Fearful in strange situations. May further develop habits with comfort objects — "security blanket".

Parental Support and Encouragement

1. Praise toddler for good behavior, but don't overdo.
2. Encourage language development by reading books to the toddler, singing, talking about what you are doing and seeing. Allow him some cardboard books to turn pages by 'self'.
3. Encourage (SAFE) exploration and initiative.
4. Encourage the toddler to play alone (he'll need some structure/check-in time) as well as with playmates, siblings and parents.
5. To set limits for a toddler, use distraction, gentle restraint, removal of object from toddler or, if you believe in it and can do it calmly, time out.
6. Limit number of rules and avoid unnecessary conflict situations by heading off trouble before it starts. Structure really helps.
7. Maintain a regular bedtime. Will make it through some nights completely.
8. Discuss toilet training with your healthcare professional.
9. TV still has nothing much to offer infants compared with human interaction.

With contributions from Dr. Kyle Pruett, Yale University

First and Second Years

Physical Development	Motor Skills	Adaptive Development	Social Development
The usual weight gain in this period is 4 to 6 pounds. Average growth is 4 to 5 inches. May have daytime bowel control.	Walks without help. Is very mobile, will start to climb stairs, at first by creeping and then with two feet on each step. Will learn to run, at first falling often. As he/she gains more balance, he assumes standing position without help. Will learn to stop suddenly without falling, can pick up objects and kick and throw a ball. Toddler likes to push and pull toys. Seats self in chair. Uses a cup. Scribbles spontaneously. Can build tower of 6 or 7 blocks. Can turn doorknob and unscrew lids.	Able to identify some shapes. Displays intense interest in pictures. Will develop a spoken vocabulary during this period of around 300 words. Understands 1 or 2 directional commands. Refers to self by name. Often talks incessantly.	Tolerates some separation from parent. Expresses emotions, hugs and kisses parents and has temper tantrums. Open drawers and doors to find objects. Is a great imitator. Beginning awareness of ownership. Has some sense of time; waits in response to "just a minute". Dresses self in simple clothes.

Parental Support and Encouragement

1. Praise toddler for good behavior, but don't overdo.
2. Encourage language development by reading books, singing, talking about what you are doing and seeing.
3. Reinforce self-care and self-expression.
4. To promote a sense of competence and control, invite the toddler to make simple choices whenever possible.
5. Encourage the toddler to be assertive in appropriate situations.
6. Decide what limits are important to you and your toddler. Briefly tell your toddler why she is being disciplined. Attempt to be as consistent as possible when enforcing limits. Keep it short and sweet.
7. When disciplining, make a verbal separation between him/her and his/her behavior: "I love you, but I don't like it when you…"
8. When possible, give a toddler a "yes" as well as a "no" (you can not play with the vase, you can play with the blocks).

—continued

With contributions from Dr. Kyle Pruett, Yale University

First and Second Year Parental Support and Encouragement —continued

9. Do not get into a power struggle with your child. Sidestep conflict and assert your power calmly and swiftly. You can control only your own responses to the toddler's behavior. For example, you cannot make a toddler sleep. But you can insist she stay in his/her room.

10. Recognize that toilet training is part of a developmentally appropriate learning. Delay training until the toddler is dry for periods of about two hours, knows the difference between wet and dry, can pull his pants up, wants to learn and gives a signal when he is about to have a bowel movement.

11. Spend individual time with the child, playing with him, hugging or holding him, taking walks, painting, and doing puzzles together.

12. Appreciate the child's investigative nature, and do not excessively limit this.

13. Promote physical activity in a safe environment.

14. Encourage parallel play with other children; do not expect shared play yet.

15. Use time out or remove source of conflict for unacceptable behavior.

16. Prepare strategies to deal with night awakening, night fears, nightmares, and night terrors.

With contributions from Dr. Kyle Pruett, Yale University

Third Year

Physical Development	Motor Skills	Adaptive Development	Social Development
Usually will have gained 4 to 6 pounds and grow approx. 3 inches. Will occasionally have night time control of bowel and bladder.	Rides tricycle. Jumps off bottom stair. Stands on one foot. Goes up stairs alternating feet. Tries to dance. Can draw circles and crosses. Builds towers and bridges with blocks.	Has a spoken vocabulary of about 900 words. Uses complete sentences with three or four words. May talk constantly. Dresses self almost completely. Feeds self. Can help with small one or two staged tasks. May have fear of dark or going to bed. Begins to work out social interaction though play. Talks to dolls, animals, trucks, etc. More able to share, wait turn.	Is still self-centered in thought and behavior. Has beginning ability to view concepts from another's perspective. Usually attempts to please parents and conform to their expectations. Is aware of family relationships and sex roles. Boys usually identify with father, family males and girls with mother, family females.

Parental Support and Encouragement

1. Praise the child for good behavior and accomplishment.
2. Encourage the child to talk with you about his/her preschool, friends, and observations. Can answer simple, non-judgmental questions.
3. Encourage interactive reading with the child. Be patient—they adore repetition often beyond adult tolerance.
4. Spend individual time with the child whenever possible.
5. Provide opportunities for the three-year-old to socialize with other children.
6. Recognize that toilet training is part of a developmentally appropriate learning. Delay toilet training until the toddler is dry for periods of about two hours, knows the difference between wet and dry, can pull his pants up, wants to learn and gives a signal when he is about to have a bowel movement.
7. Promote physical activity and play.
8. Reinforce limits and appropriate behavior.
9. Give child opportunities to make choices.
10. Limit TV to an average of an hour a day of appropriate, educational, non-adult programming. Watch with them.

With contributions from Dr. Kyle Pruett, Yale University

Fourth Year

Physical Development	Motor Skills	Adaptive Development	Social Development
Usually will have gained 4 to 6 pounds and grow approx. 3 inches.	Skips and hops on one foot. Catches and throws a ball. Uses scissors successfully. Can draw squares and stick figures.	Has a vocabulary of about 1500 words. Uses complete sentences with three or four words. Talks constantly. Questioning is at its peak. Tells exaggerated stories. Knows simple songs. Understands "under", "on top of", "beside", "in back" or "in front of". Repeats four digits. Often loves to help cook, clean, put laundry away.	Quite independent. Tends still to be selfish, impatient, and aggressive. Boasts tattles and tells family tales with little restraint. Still has many fears. (thunder, dogs) Imaginary friends are common. Works through unresolved conflict (with help). Understands time better, especially in terms of sequence of daily events. May count but has poor math concepts. Takes aggression and frustration out on parents and siblings. Do's and don'ts become important.

Parental Support and Encouragement

1. Praise the child for good behavior and accomplishment, but don't exaggerate-the outside world won't.
2. Encourage the child to talk with you about his/her preschool, friends, observations—the good and the less good. Answer questions.
3. Encourage interactive reading with the child.
4. Spend individual time with the child whenever possible.
5. Provide opportunities for socialization with other children.
6. Promote physical activity of all kinds.
7. Reinforce limits and appropriate behavior.
8. Give child opportunities to make choices, be creative, participate in generous and giving acts in family and neighborhood.
9. Limit TV to an average of an hour a day of appropriate, educational, non-adult programming. Watch with them!
10. Encourage assertiveness without aggression.
11. Enlarge the child's experiences.

With contributions from Dr. Kyle Pruett, Yale University

Fifth Year

Physical Development	Motor Skills	Adaptive Development	Social Development
May begin getting permanent teeth. Have usually established hand preference.	Skips and hops on alternate feet. Catches and throws a ball. Jumps ropes and skates. Ties shoes. Prints a few letters, numbers and words.	Has a vocabulary of about 2500 words. Uses complete sentences. Names coins, colors, days of week, months. Asks meaning of words. Asks inquisitive questions. Can do all self care.	Is more settled and eager to get down to business. Is independent and more trustworthy. Relies on outer authority to control their world. Likes rules and tries to play by them but may cheat to avoid losing. Begins to notice the outside world and is curious to where/how he belongs. Enjoys doing activities with parent of same sex.

Parental Support and Encouragement

1. Praise the child for cooperation and accomplishment.
2. Encourage the child to talk with you about his/her school or friends. May help to prime the pump by telling him/her a little about yours.
3. Encourage the child to express his/her feelings.
4. Encourage interactive reading with the child. Daily.
5. Spend individual time with the child doing something you both enjoy.
6. Enhance the child's breadth of experience. Take on something new to BOTH of you.
7. Provide opportunities to interact with other children.
8. Help the child learn to get along with peers. Set appropriate examples in your own social behavior.
9. Promote physical activities of all kinds, continue to limit TV.
10. Expect the child to follow family rules, such as those for bedtime, TV, and chores.
11. Teach the child the difference between right and wrong, respect for authority, anger management.
12. Assign age appropriate chores.
13. Introduce to computer use at home or library.

With contributions from Dr. Kyle Pruett, Yale University

Sixth and Seventh Years

Physical Development	Motor Skills	Adaptive Development	Social Development
Height and weight gain slow, average growth 2 inches and 5 pounds. Wisdom teeth begin. Gradual increase in activity to constant. Still uses fingers when eating. Loves to practice new physical skills. Likes to draw, print and color.	Enjoys practicing new language, memory and math skills. Counts 13 pennies. Knows whether it is morning or afternoon. Defines common objects such as "fork" and "chair" in terms of use. Obeys triplet commands in succession. Says which is pretty and which is ugly when looking at pictures. Reads from memory, enjoys oral spelling games. Likes to boast.	At table, uses knife to spread butter or jam. At play, cuts, folds, pastes paper. Enjoys making simple figures in clay or play dough. Takes a bath without supervision, performs bedtime activities alone. Likes table games, checkers, and simple card games. Influenced by school friends. Has own way of doing things. Tries out own abilities.	Can share and cooperate better. Has strong need for play with peers. Often engages in rough play. Is often jealous of younger brother and sister. Does what he/she sees adults doing good or bad. Often has frustration. Likes to boast. Will cheat to win. Has difficulty owning up to misdeeds. Sometimes steals money or attractive items and then lies.

Parental Support and Encouragement

1. Praise your child for cooperation and accomplishments.
2. Encourage your child to talk about school, friends or observations by listening carefully and remembering what they say. Answer their questions.
3. Encourage your child to express his or her feelings, and help by appropriately expressing yours.
4. Encourage reading - both alone and together.
5. Spend individual time with your child, something both of you enjoy.
6. Enlarge your child's experiences through family trips and outings.
7. Help your child to learn how to get along with peers.
8. Help your child learn how to follow group rules.
9. Promote daily physical activity in a safe environment and monitor TV habits.
10. Set limits and establish consequences for misbehavior.
11. Encourage self-discipline and impulse control.
12. Expect your child to follow family rules, such as those at bedtime, television viewing and chores.
13. Teach your child to respect authority by being a respectful authority.
14. Foster your child's ability to communicate with you, teachers and other adults by going to school.
15. Make sure your child understands the difference between right and wrong.
16. Teach your child how to manage anger and resolve conflicts without physical or emotional violence.

With contributions from Dr. Kyle Pruett, Yale University

Eighth and Ninth Years

Physical Development	Motor Skills	Adaptive Development	Social Development
Continues to grow 2 inches and gain about 6 pounds a year. Always on the go: jumps, chases and skips. Increased smoothness and speed in the motor control. Movement fluid; often graceful and poised. Dresses self completely with predictable personal style. Eyes and hands are well coordinated.	Attends third and fourth grade. Gives similarities and differences between two things from memory. Repeats days of the week and months in order. Counts backward from 20. Makes change out of a quarter. Reads classic books and enjoys comics. Is more aware of time; can be relied on to get to school on time. Is afraid of failing a grade; ashamed of bad grades, mistakes.	Makes use of common tools such as hammer, saw, house-hold utensils. Helps with household tasks. Looks after all of own needs at table. Exercises some choice in making purchases. Goes about community freely. Great reader likes pictorial magazines. Enjoys school. Likely to overdo; hard to quiet down after recess.	Easy to get along with at home; better behaved. Likes the reward system. Dramatizes often. Is more sociable. Is better 'behaved' by adult standards. Interested in boy-girl relationships but will not admit it. Likes to compete & play games. Is more critical of self. Has developed a personal style. Knows right from wrong and can dispense crude justice.

Parental Support and Encouragement

1. Serve as a positive ethical, moral and behavioral role model.
2. Contribute to the child's self-esteem by honoring his/her effort and showing affection.
3. Show interest in the child's school performance and activities by visiting school and being aware of projects. Display work at home.
4. Set reasonable but challenging expectations.
5. Promote self-responsibility.
6. Show affection and respect in the family.
7. Spend some individual time with each child.
8. Participate in games and physical activities with the child.
9. Encourage positive interactions between the child, parents and siblings.
10. Share meals as a family whenever possible, and encourage child to help in preparation.
11. Know the child's friends and their families.
12. Handle anger constructively in the family.
13. Spend time talking to each other.
14. Teach your child how to manage anger and resolve conflicts without physical or emotional violence.

With contributions from Dr. Kyle Pruett, Yale University

Tenth Through Eleventh Years

Physical Development	Motor Skills	Adaptive Development	Social Development
Slow growth in height and rapid weight gain, may become obese during this period if passive. Posture is more similar to an adult's. Pubescent changes may begin to appear, especially in females as body lines soften and round out. Rest of teeth will erupt and tend toward full development.	Attend fifth and sixth grades. Writes occasional short letters to friends or relative on own initiative. Uses phone/computer for practical purposes. Responds to magazines, TV or other advertising by mailing coupons. Reads for practical information or own enjoyment.	Does occasional or brief work on own initiative around home and neighborhood. Is sometimes left alone at home for short periods of time. Is successful in looking after own needs or those of other children left in care briefly. Cooks and sews in small way. Does easy repair. Cares for pets. Writes brief stories, simple paintings or drawings. Washes and dries own hair but may need reminding to do so.	Likes family; family really has meaning. Likes mother and wants to please her. Demonstrates affection. Dad is adored and idolized. (Enjoy it while it lasts!) Loves friends, talks about them constantly. Chooses friends more selectively. Beginning to take an interest in the opposite sex. Is more diplomatic. Can discuss moral choices when facing right vs. wrong decisions.

Parental Support and Encouragement

1. Anticipate wide range of pre-adolescent behaviors including the strong influence of peers, a change in the communication pattern between adolescents and parents, new challenges to parental authority, conflicts over independence, refusal to participate in some family activities, moodiness, and new risk taking.
2. Serve as a positive ethical and behavioral role model.
3. Contribute to the child's self-esteem by praising him and showing affection toward him and within the family. (see above)
4. Show interest in the child's school performance/activities. Know teachers and major events. Set reasonable but challenging expectations.
5. Promote self-responsibility at and away from home.
6. Participate in games and physical activities with the child.
7. Share meals as a family whenever possible. Leave the stress at work.
8. Foster conversation and open communication in the family.
9. Know the child's friends and their families.
10. Encourage the development of good sibling relationships.
11. Discuss (and demonstrate) value/meaning of money in family and society. Discuss allowance, chores, savings, gift giving, charity, etc.
12. Teach your child how to manage anger and resolve conflicts without physical or emotional violence.

With contributions from Dr. Kyle Pruett, Yale University

Twelfth Through Fourteenth Years

Physical Development	Intellectual Development	Relationship Skills
Maximum growth increases, especially in height. Gain in height is abrupt at the onset and continues at a rapid rate the first 2 years, followed by a deceleration. Acne probable. Girls are generally 2 years ahead of boys in development at first. Beginning of menstruation (avg., age 12 1/2 yr., range 11-16). Boys experience nocturnal emissions. Coordination improves until approximately 14 when it reaches a plateau and the child may then appear awkward, especially boys. Has general anxiety about appearance and an intense pre-occupation with developing body size. Anxiety about functioning well in society and especially about being small. Struggles to master new physical capabilities. Is very self-centered. Compares "normality" with peers of same sex.	Exploring limited ability to think abstractly about culture, politics, religion, permanence of death. Tries out various roles, identities. Conforms to group norms of dress, activities and vocabulary while seeking 'individuality'. Measures attractiveness by acceptance or rejection of peers. Develops close idealized friendships with members of the same sex. Differences are intolerable to the peer group; uniformity is the norm. Struggle for mastery takes place within peer group. Effectively uses humor to criticize family and friends. Watching TV, listening to music, talking on the phone/ internet, sports and group activities are favorite past-times. Boys interest center around sports, sports figures and video games. Girls discuss boys, clothes, and makeup.	Often indecisive. Has wide mood swings, frustrates them and you. Daydreams intensely. Expresses anger outwardly with moodiness, temper outburst, verbal insults and name-calling. Attempts repeated separation from parents and concentrates on relationships with peers. Is period of highest parent-child conflict. Takes instant exception to opinion expressed by others. Forms ego ideal of male through relationships with father. Has strong desire to remain dependent on parents while trying to detach. Craves privacy.

Parental Support and Encouragement

1. Understand that the adolescent may be unwilling to participate in some family activities and may suddenly challenge parental authority.
2. Decide with the adolescent when he/she can do things on their own, including staying at home alone.
3. Establish realistic expectations for family rules, with increasing independence and responsibility given to the adolescent who has shown he/she can handle increasing doses of it.

— continued

Twelfth Through Fourteenth Years Parental Support and Encouragement — continued

4. Establish and communicate clear limits and consequences for breaking rules. Consciously use humor whenever possible.
5. Emphasize the importance of school academically and socially.
6. Enhance the adolescent's self-esteem by providing praise, reassurance and minimize criticism, nagging, sarcasm and belittling comments (and you WILL be tempted!).
7. Spend time with the adolescent, even if they don't ask for it.
8. Respect the adolescent's need for privacy both physical and emotional.
9. Discuss with child your expectations about drugs, alcohol, and respectful intimate relationships now and down the road.
10. Teach your child how to manage anger and resolve conflicts without physical or emotional violence.

With contributions from Dr. Kyle Pruett, Yale University

Fifteenth Through Seventeenth Years

Physical Development	Intellectual Development	Relationship Skills
Female attains physical maturity. Possible/probable sexual/drug/alcohol experimentation with peers and confusion over roles are possible. Masturbation is a central activity or concern, depending on individual.	Abstract thinking established. Has ability to think logically and maintain an argument. Gradually realizes that others' thoughts are not directed toward them. Worries about school work. Enjoys intellectual powers. Invest love in another, may experience the intensity of "being in love." Acceptance by peers is extremely important—fear of rejection continues. Peer group sets behavioral standards. Explores "sex appeal" power. Turns toward heterosexuality (if homosexual, may know by this time). Sports activities are important. Feels need for a car for autonomy. Has or wants outside jobs to earn money.	Is very self-centered, increased arrogance. Tends toward inner experience and self-discovery. Struggles to define attractiveness as perceived through personal appearance. Tends to withdraw when upset or hurt. Feelings of inadequacy are common; has difficulty asking for help. Low points in parent-child relationship recur, emotional detachment frequent. Greatest push for independence, causing major conflicts over independence.

Parental Support and Encouragement

1. Decide with the adolescent when she can do things on his/her own, including staying at home alone.
2. Establish realistic expectations for family rules, with increasing independence and responsibility given to the adolescent.
3. Establish and communicate clear limits and reach an agreement on appropriate consequences for breaking rules.
4. Continue to stress the importance of school, reinforcing your expectations regarding their future successes.
5. Enhance the adolescent's self-esteem by providing praise and minimize criticism, nagging and belittling comments. (see above)
6. Spend time with the adolescent. (see above)
7. Respect the adolescent's need for privacy. (see above)
8. Refresh the previous discussion about drugs, alcohol and sex, no matter how uncomfortable. Pediatricians/nurses can help with suggestions. Talk IS the anti-drug.
9. Teach your child how to manage anger and resolve conflicts without physical or emotional violence.

With contributions from Dr. Kyle Pruett, Yale University

Eighteenth Year and Up

Physical Development	Intellectual Development	Relationship Skills
Attains physical maturity in male; growth in height ceases at 18 to 20 years. More comfortable with physical growth and attractiveness. Sexual identity is generally secured. Body image and gender role definition are nearly selected.	Is capable of protecting their identity in face of diversity. Able to view complex problems more objectively, less personally. Able to make stable relationships and form attachments to another. Importance of peer groups is lessening. New depths in interpersonal relationships form. Social roles are defined and expressed. Creative imagination cools. Prefers purposeful action. Life goals and tasks are taking shape. Pursues a career or vocation and decisions about lifestyle. Is at a decisive turning point. Defines purpose in terms of life goals. Relationships with opposite sex are less self-centered.	Has a more stable, predictable emotion. Anger is more apt to be concealed. Is in phase of consolidation of identity. Stability of self-esteem occurs. Begins to think of the possibility of more permanent male-female relationship. Have fewer conflicts with family. Is independent from family. Is able to take or leave advice.

Parental Support and Encouragement

1. Encourage the older adolescent's independent decision making when appropriate.
2. Discuss his or her plans for independent living/college/job, financial realities.
3. Establish joint expectations with the adolescent regarding family rules and responsibilities.
4. Enhance the adolescent's self esteem by providing praise and recognizing positive behavior and achievements.
5. Minimize criticism, nagging, and derogatory comments.
6. Spend time with teen.
7. Respect the adolescence's need for privacy. (see above)
8. Teach your child how to manage anger and resolve conflicts without physical or emotional violence.

With contributions from Dr. Kyle Pruett, Yale University